word

Published by the Arizona Daily Star, a Lee Enterprises Newspaper
Tucson, Arizona 2012

ISBN 978-0-9607758-4-2

Cover photo by A.E. Araiza
Book design by Michael Rice

Stories researched by Arizona Daily Star news staff
Photographs taken by Arizona Daily Star photo staff
Page 75 Rita Hayworth photo: George Hurrell/John Kobal Foundation via Getty Images

Tucson Oddities, Too

ANOTHER COLLECTION OF THE SIGHTS THAT MAKE UP THE OLD PUEBLO

Whether it's a piece of art, a historic remnant, an unfinished building or folklore about Tucson, the city has plenty of odd features that pique curiosity.

Beginning in 1999 the Arizona Daily Star published a feature for several years called "What's with that?" which answered readers' questions about different things around Tucson.

In the summer of 2009, the Star brought back the series under the name "Tucson Oddity" as a weekly item. Star readers have submitted hundreds of queries and suggestions via email to oddity@azstarnet.com

In the fall of 2011, the Star presented readers with Volume I of the Tucson Oddities book. The popularity of the novelty book prompted the production of Volume II in Spring 2012.

On the cover: The two-story Tyrannosaurus rex looms over an east-side intersection.

Arizona Daily Star

TABLE OF CONTENTS

The Park Avenue Christian Church was similar to other drive-in houses of worship, which had slogans like "Come as you are, worship in your car" and "Don't drive by, drive in."

Drive-in church

OUTDOOR SUNDAY SERVICES LET CONGREGANTS USE THEIR CARS AS PEWS

After operating for 45 years, a south-side drive-in church folded in early 2011 and the remnants of the operation pique curiosity.

The Park Avenue Christian Church opened in 1952 and in 1966 added its drive-in Sunday service. The pastor would preach alongside an organist to a congregation in parked cars with speaker boxes or low-frequency FM radio broadcasts of the sermons.

The late John Coatsworth was the church's pastor from 1960 to 1982, and created the drive-in service. He held early services at drive-in movie theaters, preaching from a trailer bed using recorded music. Later on, the service moved to the church's own property. Coatsworth retired in 1982 and died in 1998. The church's property spanned about a city block on South Park Avenue, just north of Irvington Road.

Empty armor

OFFICIAL NAME IS 'FLAYED FIGURE,' AND IT'S BEEN THERE SINCE 1972

The obscure sculpture in downtown's El Presidio Park is titled "Flayed Figure," but is also called "Winged Victory."

The bronze sculpture is a human torso of sorts.

Sculptor Donald Haskin worked on it in the early 1970s.

"It's like empty armor," he told the Star in February 2011. "It wasn't intended to be figurative."

The sculpture was completed in 1972 and is one of several pieces of art that went up in downtown Tucson in the early 1970s, city officials said.

Haskin's sculpture is on the east side of the park, near the Pima County Superior Courthouse.

El Presidio Park's art collection includes other sculptures, statues, fountains and memorials. Look around — maybe you'll spot the bust of John F. Kennedy.

Hikers' underpass

ROAD TO SUBDIVISION GOES OVER IT, BUT THOSE ON TRAIL ARE SAFE

Take a hike up a desert trail into rugged Pima Canyon north of Tucson and you might be surprised.

The trail leads through a cavernous, concrete tunnel-like underpass beneath a road bridge — similar to what you might encounter while driving a highway. But you're trekking on a national forest trail.

Odd as it might appear to hikers coming upon it for the first time, the underpass serves an important purpose: providing safety.

A road leading to a subdivision crosses the trail site, and developers installed a bridge and underpass so hikers could avoid the road, county officials said.

The trailhead, at the east end of Magee Road, is on county land.

Even though this underpass is on a hiking trail, it shares a characteristic with ones that run under city streets and highways: lots of graffiti.

Names, designs, proclamations of love and other scrawls cover the curved ceiling.

In addition to keeping hikers and traffic apart, the underpass "also keeps the subdivision private," a county official said. "The hikers can't access the subdivision."

Lightning eagle

'WINGED FREEDOM' SOARS FROM STUMP OF TREE KILLED BY 1998 BOLT

In 1998, a flash of lightning blasted a pine tree at the Southern Arizona VA Health Care System on Tucson's south side.

Michael Pal, the VA's head chef, had a vision for the charred and splintered wood.

He'd carved ice sculptures for decades and used his chain saw to create a large eagle with raised wings.

The 8-foot-tall eagle sits atop a 7-foot base within the hospital's memorial park.

A plaque below the eagle identifies the sculpture as "Winged Freedom" and dedicates it to former prisoners of war.

"Please take a moment to enjoy the artwork and reflect upon the sacrifices endured by all service men and women who were taken prisoner," it reads.

In the charred remains and splintered wood of the lightning-damaged pine, hospital head chef Michael Pal saw more than just a damaged tree; he saw a symbol of freedom.

Tunguska arrived at the state building in the company of an excavated skeleton of an adult male woolly mammoth. That piece sold for nearly $100,000 to a buyer from Alaska.

Woolly resident

TUNGUSKA IS A MUSEUM-QUALITY REPLICA OF SPECIMEN FROM SIBERIA

Tunguska, the replica of a 1-year-old woolly mammoth from the Museum of Natural History in Novosibirsk, Russia, lives at the Arizona Geological Survey Map and Bookstore at 416 W. Congress St., Suite 100.

Tunguska, which has yak hair, is a museum-quality replica that is valued at $20,000.

Some 15,000 years ago, a less-hairy mammoth — the Columbian mammoth — was common during the Ice Age in the San Pedro Valley in Southern Arizona. It roamed in herds and lived off coarse grasses.

Tunguska was given its name through a contest at the Tucson Festival of Books in 2010 on the University of Arizona Mall. Around 600 people participated in the contest, and many posed for photographs with the woolly mammoth. He was named after a valley in Siberia where a meteoroid or comet exploded on June 30, 1908.

The old building, next to a former Mervyns store, is in marked contrast to the vibrant Williams Centre complex, diagonally across the intersection of East Broadway and Craycroft Road.

Midtown eyesore

ONETIME TIRE STORE HAS STOOD VACANT AT BUSY CORNER FOR DECADES

A dilapidated building at the northeast corner of East Broadway and North Craycroft Road was at one time a tire shop, but has been vacant for more than two decades.

Citizens have called for it to be razed for years. City officials, while agreeing that the corner could do without the decaying building, have not moved forward on demolishing the property.

The owners are from New York City.

In the summer of 2010, city officials told the Star a resolution was imminent.

Star of midtown

DRUGSTORE IS LONG GONE, BUT ITS ROOFTOP TRADEMARK SHINES ON

The building on the northeast corner of East Fifth Street and North Craycroft Road will always be known as Star Drug to many longtime Tucsonans.

The 10,000-square-foot building was part of a local chain of drugstores that popped up throughout Tucson between 1953 and 1986.

Star Drug might have been the most well-known because of its trademark star perched on a pole on the roof next to its drive-through window.

The star is still there, as is the drive-through bay and a marquee sign on the corner that marks the location of the long-gone Burcham Plaza, which that shopping center was once called.

Star Drug's location was last a pharmacy in the early 2000s, when it was an Osco, according to city business records. Grenier Engineering Inc. moved into the building in 2007.

The star "was probably Bob Jensen's idea," retired pharmacist Marty Ronstadt said about one of the co-owners of Defender Drug Stores, of which Star Drug was a part. "He was a very innovative guy."

"TimeCurve" is one of a pair of sculptures that used to be inside Tucson International Airport's terminal as part of the passenger-screening system.

Cultural fence

SCULPTURE NEAR AIRPORT CELEBRATES SOUTHWEST'S VARIED ACTIVITIES

At first glance, the structure sitting on the dirt berm facing South Country Club Road, past Los Reales Road, looks like nothing more than a copper and green fence.

A closer look reveals a hard hat, shovel, a couple of irons and a basket lodged inside the fence.

The fence is an 80-foot-long sculpture titled "TimeCurve" and consists of a green metal cage filled with objects that represent Southwestern culture, Tucson Airport Authority officials said.

The sculpture used to be inside the airport, serving as a divider between arriving- and departing-passenger areas on the east concourse.

It was created by artist Barbara Grygutis and architect Page Cotton in 1995.

Airport officials removed the sculpture in 2007 and put it in storage during a concourse-expansion project. "TimeCurve" has been at its new home, which is on the road leading to the airport's garage, since the summer of 2010.

"I like the coyotes a lot," homeowner Mike Soderberg said. "They are the only thing in my front yard that are not plain or boring."

Palm tree coyotes

DEAD TREES WERE BROUGHT BACK TO NEW LIFE AS DESERT CREATURES

The trunks of two dead palm trees have another life form as sculptures of howling coyotes.

The figures — one about 5 feet tall and the other about 4 feet tall — flank a live palm tree that juts some 30 feet into the air at an east-side house in the El Dorado Hills subdivision, near East Speedway and North Wilmot Road. The house sits on the corner of Rosewood Circle and North Caribe Avenue.

The homeowner said he gets requests from people passing by to take photos with the sculptures. Neighbors have told him the coyotes were sculpted out of the palm trees that withered and died about a decade ago.

The then-homeowner had the tree trunks cut down and commissioned an artist by the surname of Youngblood to create the coyote sculptures.

Perpetual play

SCULPTURE WENT TO RILLITO PARK WHEN RADIO STATION DIDN'T WANT IT

A tall steel sculpture titled "People Play" keeps company with mesquite trees and barrel cacti near the soccer fields at Rillito Park, on North First Avenue just south of River Road.

The 30-foot-tall sculpture is a tower of several parabolic arches stacked atop and looping through each other.

Sixteen figures of nude men and women with varying expressions of joy carved on their faces are posed on the arches.

The metalwork, made by Thomas Bredlow, was originally commissioned by Steve Nanini and was installed in front of one of his former properties at 7355 N. Oracle Road.

In the early 1990s when Family Life Radio took over the building, the station removed the sculpture, saying it did not fit in with its landscape plans.

A representative from the Christian station said the organization wanted to install a flagpole in place of the sculpture. The artwork was installed at Rillito Park in 1992.

Artist Thomas Bredlow wanted the work moved to the entrance of a landfill so people could enjoy the sculpture as they came and went, and when the dump filled up, it would be the last thing tossed in.

Odd antenna

IT HELPS PROVIDE EARLY WARNING ON FLOODING, NOT A TV SIGNAL

Drivers on the Sabino Canyon Road bridge over Tanque Verde Creek sometimes do a double take when they spot an antenna perched above the bridge.

What could it be?

Some kind of high-tech traffic sensor that might lead to a speeding ticket? An inter-galactic listening device waiting for a call from E.T.?

A TV receiver put up by some homeless guy living under the bridge?

No. It's an antenna used to transmit data on rainfall and stream-flow levels.

Information from the site — and more than 90 others around Southern Arizona — helps authorities provide early warnings about pos-sible flooding.

Data from a rain gauge and a stream-flow gauge go to a transmitter, and the radio anten-na sends the information to offices of the Pima County Flood Control District and the National Weather Service.

"We're really proud of our system," a county hydrologist said. "It's very crucial during limited times of the year" — like during the monsoon.

"It's definitely not a Joesler," business owner Bruce Fairchild said, referring to Josias Joesler, a famed local architect in the first half of the 20th century. "We just call it the upside-down arches."

Regal rooftop

A VARIETY OF BUSINESSES HAVE WORN 1950S BUILDING'S CROWN

Built in 1957, the storefront with the spindly top may be the only one of its kind in Tucson, the Tucson Historic Preservation Foundation believes.

Located at 2635 E. Broadway, the crown-like roof sits over Safes Unlimited, a safe and locksmith business.

Commerce blossomed along that stretch of East Broadway after World War II, and by the 1950s it was home to an important shopping corridor known as the Sunshine Mile.

The store with the strange roof was first occupied by Wheeler's TV and Appliance Store, which, in 1957, sold Whirlpool automatic washing machines, among other things.

By the late 1960s, Wheeler's had moved out, and two electronics businesses moved in. The safe and locksmith business has been there for about 15 years.

Vandals were a constant problem for owners Della and Walter Willcox at their would-be amusement park, which sat on what was then the main road from Tucson to Mexico.

'God's Little Acre'

AMUSEMENT PARK THAT NEVER HAPPENED SITS SOUTH OF TUCSON

A property along South Nogales Highway holds remnants of one of the region's first unofficial adopt-a-road cleanup programs.

About five miles south of Valencia Road lies what's left of "God's Little Acre," a collection of sculptures and structures made from rock and glass bottles collected along Nogales Highway.

It was conceived as a fantasy-style amusement park by the land's original owners, Della and Walter Willcox, who bought the acre in 1946 after moving from Arkansas.

The park never came to fruition, according to a 1973 Arizona Daily Star story. Walter died in 1954, but Della continued to try to build. There's a stone house at the front of the property, as well as numerous fountains and tables, a castle-like doghouse and the shell of what once was a country store.

Della died in 1981 at age 82.

One cool cat

WILBUR'S A WILDCAT THROUGH AND THROUGH, SO JUST IGNORE THE TAIL

Of all the world's cats, Wilbur — the University of Arizona mascot — is a creature unto himself. With the face of a bobcat, the tail of a cougar and the fashion sense of a college student, Wilbur is his own tom.

UA teams earned their nickname, the Wildcats, after a hard-fought football game against the Occidental College Tigers on Nov. 7, 1914. A Los Angeles Times columnist wrote that the Arizona team "showed the fight of wildcats," according to the university website.

The school used live bobcats until the late 1950s when two students suggested the school mascot take the form of a costumed human. Wilbur Wildcat made his first appearance in 1959.

When Wilbur took the field he had the head of a bobcat and the tail of a mountain lion.

University officials could not explain his parentage and said Wilbur has always been referred to simply as a wildcat.

Wilbur has been on the job for more than 50 years with his fuzzy, bobcatty face and a long tail he swings like a lariat — his signature move.

The chicken's perch is a ramshackle roost, with rusted metal and peeling paint dating back half a century or so, but sightseers still stop by to snap photos of the old eatery sign.

Grinning fowl

CHICKEN IS ONE OF A COUPLE OF ADDITIONS TO SIGN SPORTING ATOM

From his perch along Interstate 10's eastbound off ramp and South Sixth Avenue, a grinning chicken with a gold tooth rules the roost.

It once was the logo for a Mr. Quick hamburger stand at the northeast edge of Southgate Shopping Center in the 1960s.

No one seems sure when the chicken's likeness was added, though some neighbors vaguely recall a takeout chicken store occupying the former burger joint during the 1980s.

The building also was formerly home to El Indio restaurant, and to a Chuy's restaurant.

The sign is historically significant, a member of the Tucson-Pima County Historical Commission and advocate for the preservation of old signage said.

The atom on top is one of the last surviving examples of a popular 1950s style of signage known as Googie, which favored futuristic shapes such as stars, rocket ships, atoms or satellites.

"Steel is my clay," said artist Bruce Butler, who began creating such sculptures in 1990. "I can do some pretty interesting techniques and textures with things."

Chief Many Moons

MENACING STEEL MAN STANDS GUARD AT NORTHWEST-SIDE RESIDENCE

Three of local sculptor Bruce Butler's rusted-steel sculptures can be found at a home on the west side of North La Cañada Drive between West River and West Orange Grove roads, including the stern-looking Chief Many Moons.

The works are among dozens the lifelong Tucsonan has made since developing his technique of molding metal into monolithic art.

The works are as intriguing as their creator.

Butler has been a schoolteacher, painter, photographer and even a model.

He was the International Camel Man for Camel cigarettes from 1984 to 1986, before being replaced by the cartoon Joe Camel character.

A number of the sculptures are modeled after historical American Indian and Wild West characters.

Saguarohenge

CACTUS CIRCLE AT PIMA PARKS OFFICE A TRIBUTE TO BUILDER'S MOTHER

Eight skinny saguaros form a circle on a knoll in Pima Prickly Park at 3500 W. River Road.

Robie Pardee planted Saguarohenge sometime in the early 2000s as a tribute to his mother, Alice Pike Pardee.

At the time, Pardee worked for Pima County as a project manager and was responsible for landscaping the Parks Department's new headquarters, which opened in 2002.

Pardee, 61, died in June 2011. He was retired at the time of his death.

The saguaros were transplanted from an area near Crooked Tree Golf Course at Arthur Pack Park.

Co-workers remember Pardee's love for his mother, who was a teacher and emphasized proper grammar for her son. Alice Pardee died in 1993.

County officials plan to add boulders to the Saguarohenge site so visitors can sit and enjoy the tranquillity.

"It's quasi-spiritual being on that hill inside that circle of saguaros," said Jessie Byrd, project coordinator for Pima Prickly Park.

Botanical mystery

JUST WHAT IS THAT TOPPING THAT TREE, AND HOW DID IT GET THERE?

Something odd tops the tree on the northeast corner of Grant Road and Cherry Avenue.

City officials have looked at it with binoculars and believe it's a vine.

Someone was hired to climb the tree, but it was too flimsy to support his weight.

A conservation advocate with the Center for Biological Diversity ruled out a nest.

Biologists don't think it's a pathogen, because the tangled mass is dead, and typically such nefarious masses of growth remain living.

Based on a broken-off remnant of trunk poking up above the mass, biologists believe that a blast of wind sheared off the top of the tree, which remained on top and ultimately turned upside down and collapsed into itself.

Sometime in the next decade, the house is likely to be demolished to accommodate the Grant Road widening project. The mystery could be solved then.

People have taken pictures of the tree's strange topper. They've stopped to ask what the heck it is. "I just tell them to use their imagination," homeowner Susan Chambers Casteloes said.

A pirate ship built from an assortment of, ah, gently used second-hand items was a seasonal addition to the imposing collection for a recent Halloween.

Treasured trash

ALL MANNER OF JUNK GIVES NORTH-SIDE YARD A LOOK ALL ITS OWN

For north-side resident Gary Morrow, all manner of junk is his treasure. He's been collecting it for years and incorporating it into the wall around his house at 3674 N. Park Ave.

The creation began as a cinder-block wall put up five years ago when his truck was broken into.

Morrow has since stuccoed over the blocks and painted it to look like the Catalina Mountains.

Over the years he's added an airplane made from tennis rackets, saguaros made from drainage pipes and studded with glass beads; and an Anasazi village carved from the cliff-like stucco, which Morrow calls "Spirit Mountain."

There's a small cave carved into the wall that houses a miniature Western town.

The wall has made Morrow's house somewhat of a tourist destination. He's filled three guest books with kind notes and signatures from out-of-town visitors.

The statue is a replica of the one that stands in the U.S. Capitol as part of the National Statuary Hall Collection. The original casting of Greenway was given to the collection in 1930.

Famous sculptor

MAN WHO CARVED MOUNT RUSHMORE ALSO CREATED STATUE IN TUCSON

Sculptor Gutzon Borglum's most famous work is seen on Mount Rushmore in South Dakota: the colossal heads of four U.S. presidents.

But another one of his creations resides outside the Arizona History Museum, 949 E. Second St., next to the University of Arizona campus: A statue of John Campbell Greenway, an Alabama-born mining engineer who built the town of Ajo.

Greenway's son, Jack, helped bring his father's bronze figure to the museum.

The younger Greenway donated $50,000 to the Arizona Historical Society to landscape the grounds as a memorial to his father and his mother, Isabella Greenway King.

The statue was erected in front of the museum on May 16, 1974.

In addition to his mining career, Greenway rode with Teddy Roosevelt and the Rough Riders, worked as an executive for steel and railroad companies throughout Arizona, and served for one year as a member of the Board of Regents.

Cactus takes a bow

IT'S TWISTED, BUT ALIVE AND WELL AND WELCOMES GUESTS TO MOTEL

One very polite saguaro — which is about 12 feet tall and visible from westbound Interstate 10 — stands in front of the Travel Inn on the north side of I-10, near South Wilmot Road.

Part of the saguaro is bent downward, pointing toward the motel entrance. An arm goes straight up.

The motel's manager said the cactus greets guests and has been in that position for more than 15 years.

From a distance, the cactus may look broken or even dead, but it is alive and healthy.

Seasonal birds visit, making one of the saguaro's arms a temporary home. Visitors always do a double take and many take photos with the welcoming saguaro.

A biologist with Saguaro National Park said the bowing cactus may be that way because of damage from a freeze.

There are some saguaros in the national park that look like they're embracing, waving a hand or bending over.

"Because (saguaros) look a little bit like people, we tend to give them human attributes; that's one of the reasons they're so popular," a Saguaro National Park biologist said.

The city is unlikely to take any action on the structure unless it becomes a safety issue. "It appears to be sturdy and substantial, not falling down, and it's completely closed off," a city official said.

Unfinished business

NO ONE CAN REMEMBER WHY CONSTRUCTION WAS HALTED, OR WHEN

A brick structure on the northeast corner of North Stone Avenue and Roger Road has been half built with exposed rods of rebar jutting skyward for as long as anyone can remember.

It sits at 4002 N. Stone Ave., attached to a mattress store painted bright yellow. Best Mattress Inc., a family-owned company, owns the property.

A permit for the furniture store and the still-incomplete building was issued in the 1970s, city records show. But there's nothing in the city file indicating why construction on the building stopped.

A man in the furniture store declined to discuss the building's state with the Star. .

Kafe owner Evangelos Vassious' collection of farming equipment was once five times what it is today. "I've had lots of them stolen," he said.

Farm décor

OLD STUFF RULES AT OLD TIMES KAFE, AND HAS FOR A QUARTER-CENTURY

The owner of Old Times Kafe prefers décor straight off the farm.

Since the mid-1980s, Evangelos Vassious has collected plows and other farming equipment to display outside his restaurant at 1485 W. Prince Road.

Vassious opened the restaurant in 1986 when he moved from Greece to his wife Ina's hometown of Tucson.

"Somebody brought a load of stuff from Missouri and we bought it all and put it around for décor," Ina said in 2011.

Evangelos has also picked up equipment at auctions and from his customers.

His collection started because he wanted Old Times Kafe to have an antique look.

The inside of the restaurant also is decorated with antiques.

Royal residence

SW-SIDE CASTLE HAS IT ALL, FROM A DUNGEON TO A DRAWBRIDGE

Atop a hill near West Ajo Way and South Mission Road sits a home fit for royalty.

Built in the 1980s by the late Pat Bruno, the Mollohan Castle is dedicated to King Richard and Queen Frances of Bruno, believed to be the builder's parents.

A dungeon, accessible by a trapdoor in the kitchen, makes up the lower level of the castle. A kitchen, a living room, a bedroom and a bathroom are on the second level and another bedroom is on the third level. A domed, circular room with windows all the way around tops off the multilevel abode. A hand-painted mural of famous castles adorns the dome's ceiling. A drawbridge can be opened and closed and a trench, built for a moat, is in front of the house.

Daniel and Barbara Reese, who bought the home in 1996, told the Star in 2011 that they hoped to turn it into a bed and breakfast.

The current owners have heard stories about the late Pat Bruno, who built the place, including that the design may have been inspired by the castle from "Disney's Adventures of the Gummi Bears."

Tribute to water

EARTH COATING CONCRETE FORMS CAME FROM BOTTOM OF WASH

On the south side of Tanque Verde Road, just east of Catalina Highway, five curved concrete forms coated with dirt and rocks stand in a circle.

Each of the trough-shaped pieces was cast from the Bonanza Wash — the sculpture's earth coating came directly off the bottom of the channel.

Pima County officials said it's an impression of the actual wash.

The $170,000 sculpture stands 20 feet tall and is a tribute to water — the very reason a community developed there — says a narrative describing the sculpture's concept.

Thomas Sayre, an artist based in Raleigh, N.C., laid rebar directly in the wash, then poured concrete to form the core of each piece. The finished pieces were lifted out with a crane and installed along Tanque Verde just outside The Lakes at Castle Rock, a gated subdivision.

The Bonanza Wash was rerouted as part of the widening of Tanque Verde Road, and nearby residents wanted a sculpture that would remind them of the landscape.

George Rosenberg, the school's original director of admissions, said he believed the name was suggested by the Rev. Charles Polzer to honor Pope Gregory the Great, the patron saint of education.

Pope with no church

DESPITE ST. GREGORY NAME, SCHOOL HAS NO RELIGIOUS AFFILIATION

There is nothing intrinsically odd about St. Gregory or the college preparatory school that bears his name in Tucson. But the campus on the Rillito is nonsectarian, nondenominational and, in fact, not a religious school at all.

School officials explain that one of the school's founders had sought affiliation with the Episcopal Church but was turned down for unknown reasons.

A reverend suggested naming the school for Pope Gregory the Great, known as the patron saint of education.

At its opening the school had a Jewish director of admissions, a Lutheran chaplain and an Episcopalian priest as head.

The school has not had a chaplain since 1985.

Its website states: "We have been serving Arizona families since 1980.

"We have no religious affiliation (although we are named for the patron saint of education), and we are committed to serving a diversity of families."

Other structures, like classrooms and administrative offices, also sat on the site at one point. The only remaining evidence of those are some asphalt patches in the desert.

Old shooting range

POLICE RECRUITS SHARPENED THEIR AIM NEAR SILVERBELL GOLF COURSE

On the west side of Tucson, just south of Silverbell Golf Course, an abandoned, yellow-hued tower sits in a pit across from a lattice-covered canopy.

The property, between North Silverbell Road and the Santa Cruz River, is owned by the city.

Officials with the Tucson Police Department said it was a shooting range for the training academy up until the late 1990s.

The yellowish structure was the control tower, and recruits would fire their guns toward the large dirt berm in the opposite direction. The latticelike canopy held plywood at an angle for shade.

Other structures, like classrooms and administrative offices, also sat on the site at one point. A ramada still stands just south of the shooting range.

TPD stopped using the location once it built its new training academy on South Wilmot Road across from the state prison complex.

Moon tree

SEEDS THAT FLEW ON APOLLO 14 GREW INTO SYCAMORE ON UA CAMPUS

Trees aren't known for their extraterrestrial travel.

A notable exception is the "moon tree" on the University of Arizona campus.

It grew from seeds that traveled to the moon on the Apollo 14 flight in 1971 as part of an experiment.

The American sycamore tree — growing just east of the Flandrau science center — germinated successfully after its lunar journey.

Studies found that seeds of the sycamore, and seeds of other tree species on the Apollo flight, germinated as successfully as control seeds that never left Earth.

The UA's moon tree, one of many growing around the nation, was planted on campus as a seedling in 1976 and was designated the Bicentennial Moon Tree.

"The tree not only represents significant beauty, but it's also a part of our research and education mission," said Tanya Quist, director of the UA Campus Arboretum.

"We would not have painted it that color on purpose," a facilities management supervisor for the city of Tucson said of the police service center's unexpected hue.

Cops' soft side

STATION'S SIGN STARTED OUT RED, BUT TUCSON SUN HAD OTHER IDEAS

Pink isn't normally a color associated with policing.

But, for a while, the official signage outside Tucson's west-side cop shop was about the same shade as a flamingo.

The sign started out bright red in 2008 when the Police Service Center opened at Miracle Mile and Flowing Wells Road.

But desert sunshine took its toll, fading the original paint job, city officials said.

At first, officials thought it might have been repainted by someone in solidarity with the fight against breast cancer.

But a city official's visit to the site confirmed the more-likely suspicion that the once-crimson paint job had been bleached by sunlight.

Red paint doesn't tend to last long in Tucson. It has since been painted a neutral tan color.

"The phone booths are part of the lobby landscape, and we would never take them out even though people nowadays use cellphones," said Hotel Congress co-owner Shana Oseran.

Historic phone calls

BOOTHS IN HOTEL CONGRESS ARE MAHOGANY, ANTIQUES, AND STILL WORK

Among the odd treasures at Hotel Congress, 311 E. Congress St., are the antique mahogany telephone booths standing side by side in the lobby. The hotel was built in 1919.

The working telephone booths have mahogany swivel chairs, working fans and lights that turns on when the door is shut.

There was a fire at the hotel in 1934, so it's unclear if the booths are from 1919.

The late Vince Szuda frequented the booths daily in search of coins to add to his jars. He also gathered coins from the jukebox inside the hotel's Tap Room bar. He was among 12 people who lived at the hotel in the 1980s.

In 1965, Szuda traveled from Chicago to Tucson by train and made Hotel Congress his home. The Army veteran's military tag is embedded in the wooden bar at the Tap Room.

Numerous jars filled with coins were found in Room 220 after Szuda died on Feb. 18, 2001. He was 84.

The remote site in the Tucson Mountains is now a party spot and a magnet for graffiti. "That is my single worst area for vandalism in the entire park," Tucson Mountain Park's manager said.

A little castle

EVIDENCE INDICATES A LAWYER ORIGINALLY FROM DALLAS PUT IT THERE

The ruins of an old stone house sit atop a desert hill just north of where West 36th Street ends in a parking lot and splinters into trails through Tucson Mountain Park.

The ground in and around the roofless structure glitters with broken bottles; graffiti coats the walls and staircase.

Frederick C. Frick, who lives in Wisconsin, bought the land in 1973, records show.

"The locals called it the little castle, and I was always kind of proud to think that I bought a little castle," Frick, then 87, said in a 2011 telephone interview.

Carved into the concrete near one of the entrances reads: "Homesteaded April-21-1928," and the signature "W. Fred Kain." Bureau of Land Management records show a W. Fred Kain homesteaded land in Pima County around that time. A death certificate shows a person named William Fred Kain was born in Dallas in 1884 and moved to Tucson in 1913. It lists his occupation as attorney. He died in Tucson in 1948.

The company does a bit of everything, large and small, from installing grand stone fireplaces and columns to basic garden sculptures. Giant spheres apparently are available, too.

Forthright orbs

GIANT STONE BALLS ARE MEANT TO GRAB ATTENTION, AND BOY, DO THEY

Motorists driving along East Fort Lowell Road near North Alvernon Way may find their manhood called into question.

A sprawling banner hangs between two massive stones outside Cantera Carved Stone, 3751 E. Fort Lowell Road, with the phrase: "GOT BALLS."

Brent Jones, a drafter and architectural de-signer at the stonework company, said he and his business partner, builder Monty Bartholomew, placed the stone spheres outside their business to attract curious passers-by.

They are carved from cantera stone imported from Mexico. The big one is more than 6 feet in diameter and weighs about 16,000 pounds. The other is 4 feet tall and weighs in at 8,000 pounds.

Fish cactus

JAPANESE-BORN ARTIST DESIGNED IT TO REFLECT LOVE OF DESERT, OCEAN

Where can you find fish, sea otters, starfish or an octopus hanging from a saguaro cactus?

Probably nowhere but at Jacobs Park pool, where an 8-foot-tall cactus sculpture is covered in ceramic sea creatures.

The fish cactus stands in a cordoned-off area next to the pool in the park at 1010 W. Lind St.

Artist Hirotsune Tashima grew up in Japan near the ocean in the city of Osaka. While a foreign-exchange student in Baltimore in the late 1990s, he rode his motorcycle to Arizona and saw the desert for the first time.

In 1999, he moved to Tucson and began teaching ceramics at Pima Community College. When he heard about the call to artists for this public-art project in 2004, he wanted to create something that combined the desert he loved with the ocean where he grew up.

The final product has stingrays, sea turtles, a shark and even a mini-sea lion all living on the fish cactus.

"Living in a place full of humor and jokes, I've always been interested in fun pieces, nothing too serious," said artist Hirotsune Tashima, "and this one is a fun sculpture."

The Garden of Gethsemane, installed in 1938 and rebuilt in 1946 along the Santa Cruz River west of downtown, is a popular site these days for weddings and quinceañeras.

Promise fulfilled

WWI VET CREATED RIVERSIDE SCULPTURE GARDEN AS THANKS FOR LIFE

West of downtown sits a collection of sculptures along the banks of the Santa Cruz River. The site is known as the Garden of Gethsemane.

The display was built in 1938 by Felix Lucero, a sculptor who traveled the country for 19 years constructing statues as a gift to God for sparing his life during World War I.

Lucero was critically wounded during a battle in France, and made a vow to dedicate 20 years of his life to God if he survived.

Tucson was Lucero's last stop on his sculpt-

ing tour. The Garden of Gethsemane — a replica of a similar garden near Jerusalem — became his life's work, city officials said.

The original sculptures were built in the dry riverbed of the Santa Cruz, but a flash flood washed the display away.

Lucero built a second set of statues, completing them in 1946 on the east bank of the Santa Cruz. That display was moved to its current location, on the northeast corner of West Congress Street and Bonita Avenue, in 1982.

Old Pueblo Trolley officials figured offering the boxcars as canvases for graffiti-art contest winners was a no-brainer. "We felt they would end up with graffiti on them anyway," one said.

Broadway boxcars

THEY'RE WAREHOUSES FOR TROLLEY PARTS, AND THE GRAFFITI IS LEGAL

There's a lengthy history behind the boxcars that sit on city-owned property along East Broadway near downtown.

The graffiti art splashed across the boxcars wasn't the work of vandals, Old Pueblo Trolley officials said.

They had been stored at a location at East Eighth Street and North Fifth Avenue, but they were moved to 10 N. Park Ave. in 2009.

Locked inside those boxcars are spare parts for historical trolleys now in service and for oth-er trolleys in the process of being restored.

They hold one-of-a-kind trolley parts from Belgium, Portugal and Japan.

Originally painted an off-white color, the boxcars acquired graffiti about 10 years earlier when Old Pueblo Trolley offered them up as blank canvases to winners of a graffiti-art con-test sponsored by the Governor's Office.

The boxcars were scheduled to be repainted to look more like they did in the 1950s and have since been fenced in.

Artsy stumps

WHEN TREES FELL VICTIM TO POWER LINES, CHAIN SAW STEVE STEPPED UP

Two tree stumps on North Fourth Avenue near Fourth Street were left behind when the trees were cut down because they threatened the trolley power lines.

Around 2003, Stephen Arnett, a carpenter and landscaper, also known as Chain Saw Steve, whittled down the stumps to what remains to-day — a rainbow-colored mushroom and a man and woman standing atop butterflies and holding up the Earth.

The artwork has been the target of many vandals, but the owner of the home maintains the mushroom figure and in 2011 had plans to install solar-powered lights to illuminate the work.

The taller statue originally had a girl riding on a rocket, but the city disapproved. "I had to rescue it as much as I could, and the rocket turned into butterflies," artist Stephen Arnett said.

Once Metro Water has finished drilling on the site, "they're going to put the desert growth back the way it was," said Fruchthendler Principal John Heidel. "And we'll put in small trails."

Wildlife preserve

NOT EXACTLY, BUT IT WILL BE AN OUTDOOR ENVIRONMENTAL CLASSROOM

A fenced-in patch of desert flecked with chollas and scraggly trees sits next to an elementary school.

A sign on the fence reads "wildlife preserve."

Exactly what wildlife is being preserved in the swath of desert just south of Fruchthendler Elementary School, near North Sabino Canyon and East Cloud roads, isn't readily apparent.

The property is owned by the Metropolitan Domestic Water Improvement District, docu-

ments in the Pima County Assessor's Office show.

When acquiring the property, Metro Water started working with the Tucson Unified School District to preserve some of the landscape.

TUSD sold Metro Water the 58,715-square-foot property in 2009.

School officials said the area will serve as an outdoor classroom for students to learn about the environment.

The structure might have been installed by Water Company No. 1, which once served the area. "That's what we suspect, but we can't verify it," a Tucson Water official said.

Abandoned fountain

AT LEAST IT LOOKS LIKE ONE, BUT NO ONE CAN REMEMBER WATER IN IT

A fountain-like structure has sat in a south-side neighborhood for more than 40 years.

But nobody seems to know when it arrived or what purpose the circular structure, which stands at 38 W. District St., serves.

Tucson Water acquired the lot — in the National City neighborhood near South Sixth Avenue and West Ajo Way — and the structure in 1968 from Water Company No. 1, a city water official said.

Records on the property kept by Tucson Water say nothing about a fountain.

One longtime resident recalled neighborhood children playing on it in the late 1960s and '70s.

But no one could recall a time when it flowed with water.

Dino landmark

'JURASSIC PARK' FAN, 2, INSPIRED PARENTS TO ADD DINOSAUR DECOR

It has loomed over the intersection of Grant and Tanque Verde roads since 1993.

The two-story Tyrannosaurus rex was installed by Michelle and Michael Retzer, who bought the restaurant at 6651 E. Tanque Verde Road in the mid-1990s.

A second statue, a 10-foot Maiasaura with a nest of baby dinosaurs, resides inside the restaurant's lobby.

The couple's then-2-year-old son, Garrett, was a huge dinosaur fan thanks in part to the movie "Jurassic Park," which came out that year.

The Retzers contracted with Amado-based La Reata Studios to have the creatures built and shipped to their store, at a cost of around $55,000.

The indoor dinosaur suffered a debilitating injury in its first year after some kids climbed on it and poked out the gel-like eyes.

The gel hardened and the crying appearance of the dinosaur remains as a reminder of that accident.

Got a ferocious appetite? The T. rex looming over Grant and Tanque Verde seems to. Good thing he's right next to a McDonald's restaurant.

Storied dome

IT WAS MOVED FROM EL CONQUISTADOR HOTEL TO NORTHWEST SIDE

Casa Blanca Plaza's copper dome dates back to the El Conquistador Hotel, which opened on East Broadway in 1928 and was demolished 40 years later.

Tucson's first shopping mall — El Con — opened next to the posh hotel in 1960 and eventually included a new Levy's department store on the former hotel site soon after it was razed.

Developer George N. Genematas put in a bid to buy the copper dome, and family photos from Oct. 2, 1968, show a crane placing the dome on a City Van & Storage flatbed truck.

The dome was hauled to Casa Blanca Plaza — at North Oracle and West Rudasill roads — which was developed by Genematas in the late 1960s and is still owned and operated by his children.

Genematas, an early developer of northwest Tucson, died in 2010.

Lemon juice and every copper cleaner the family could find through the years have been used to keep the dome's shine. The dome is illuminated at night.

When Casa Blanca Plaza, featuring the dome, opened in 1969, original tenants included an AJ Bayless grocery store and a Sprouse-Reitz variety store. Heard of them lately?

Padre Eusebio Francisco Kino, a 17th-century missionary, explored, farmed and introduced cattle, horses and European crops in Northern Sonora and Southern Arizona.

Father Kino marker

MEMORIAL DEDICATED IN 1936 SITS LITTLE NOTICED NEAR CITY HALL

A memorial to the Jesuit missionary Padre Eusebio Francisco Kino remains a hidden treasure to many in the Old Pueblo.

It was unveiled on March 15, 1936 — the 225th anniversary of Kino's death — and it's near City Hall at 255 W. Alameda St.

It is a sculptured plaque set in volcanic rock of Kino on a trek wearing sandals and a robe with a cape and a hat. He is accompanied by a young indigenous boy carrying a bow and arrow.

Kino was born in 1645 in Segno, Italy, and died March 15, 1711, in Magdalena, Sonora.

Professor Frank C. Lockwood, an ordained Methodist minister who came to teach at the University of Arizona, loved the history of Kino, officials with the Roman Catholic Diocese said.

Lockwood started a committee to raise money and commissioned Mahonri Young to come up with a model of the downtown sculpture. Young was the grandson of Brigham Young, the second prophet of The Church of Jesus Christ of Latter-day Saints.

Howard Hughes' land purchases in Tucson and his off-and-on, often torrid romance with film goddess Rita Hayworth (inset) led to the idea he named the area for her. It makes a nice story, at least.

Rita's ranch?

LEGEND OF ACTRESS IS FUN, BUT NAME'S LIKELY FROM A TRAIN STATION

Legend has it that Rita Ranch, on Tucson's southeast side, was named after actress Rita Hayworth by one-time beau Howard Hughes, who once owned the property.

Hughes bought leases and options for 32,000 acres near Tucson International Airport in 1951. Real estate magnate Roy P. Drachman persuaded him to build Hughes Aircraft Co.'s manufacturing plant in Tucson. Raytheon Co. purchased the company in 1997.

The eccentric billionaire built a ranch home on the property and is said to have referred to the land as "Rita's Ranch."

Hughes held on to much of the land until he died in 1976.

Although the possibility that the naming of Rita Ranch is a lasting relic from the Hughes-Hayworth romance, it may be just wishful thinking.

The Vail Preservation Society said Rita Ranch was named after Rita Station, a train station that predates the Hughes-Hayworth affair.

OV totem pole

PILLAR OF COMMUNITY MARKS ENTRANCE TO ORO VALLEY COUNTRY CLUB

One of Oro Valley's oldest neighborhoods has a totem pole that serves as its unofficial entrance.

Local artist James Savage built the sculpture in 1960 just west of North Oracle Road along West Greenock Drive, which is the main entrance to both Oro Valley Country Club and the neighborhood that has surrounded it since 1959.

The 25-foot totem pole is made from 50 U-shaped white crushed-marble blocks and includes 150 original designs that Savage incorporated into his work to look like hieroglyphics.

The images range from those of a desert motif to others representing abstract golf clubs and tennis rackets.

The letters "OVCC" are carved into the structure.

The country club's archives indicate the land used to be owned by the homeowners association. In 1997, according to the archival information, the town took control of the land to use as a trailhead for paths along the Cañada del Oro Wash.

The structure has been there since 1960, and remains a bit of a mystery — like why artist James Savage, commissioned to do a piece of art there, chose to make it a totem pole.

The Divine Mercy Chapel attracts the faithful and the curious to a rural northwest-side neighborhood, an area where water flows in irrigation ditches and people on horseback travel dirt paths.

Welcoming chapel

NW SIDE METAL CHURCH OPENED IN 2002, DRAWS PEOPLE OF ALL FAITHS

People of all faiths make their way to the tiny Divine Mercy Chapel that sits near Alicia and Reuben Islas Jr.'s home east of Interstate 10 between West Cortaro Farms and West Ina roads.

The chapel was built by the late Charles "Gringo" Miller, a welder, sculptor and artist. The chapel's doors opened on Ash Wednesday 2002.

Miller met Alicia in 2003 when she stopped at his welding shop near North Flowing Wells and West Wetmore roads and was taken by the chapel.

She became a regular visitor to the chapel and took her husband, Reuben, to visit. Also a welder, Reuben found much in common with Miller, and they became friends.

In August 2006, Miller died at the age of 65 after a long illness. He left the chapel to Alicia and Reuben.

The chapel was relocated to the couple's property, 7831-B N. St. Patrick Road, on Dec. 12, 2007. The chapel seats up to 16 people.

A county parks official said one guess is that the sign was put up by somebody who once lived in the area. And, yes, one imagines that the family name might have been Bartlett.

The Bartlett mystery

IS IT A WAY OF LIVING? A PATH TO SOMEWHERE? NO ONE SEEMS TO KNOW

It's a weathered metal sign, anchored firmly in a patch of desert barely a stone's throw from a trail in Greasewood Park.

Three words are welded onto the sign: "The Bartlett Way."

Officials from the Tucson Parks and Recreation Department say its origin is a mystery.

The sign — in an area of the park bristling with ocotillos, cacti and desert trees — can be reached in a five-minute walk from Speedway west of Greasewood Road.

To get to the sign, begin walking up an old roadbed near the intersection of Speedway and Saddlewood Ranch Drive.

Follow the old road for a hundred yards or so and watch for the sign on the left at the point where the route splits at a "Y" junction.

Reptilian ride

BRIDGE NEAR DOWNTOWN LETS BICYCLISTS FEEL LIKE A SNAKE'S LUNCH

The Rattlesnake Bridge allows pedestrians and cyclists to cross East Broadway west of Euclid Avenue. Its actual name is the Broadway Bicycle Pedestrian Bridge, and it boasts the face of a diamondback rattler with 11-foot-long fangs and a translucent tunnel, which is painted with diamond shapes.

The bridge cost $2.47 million and was completed in May 2002 after being delayed when two trucks plowed into its support structures during construction in 2001.

Local artist Simon Donovan came up with the concept for the bridge, TY Lin International designed it, and Hunter Contracting Co. handled construction.

The Federal Highway Administration granted it an Excellence in Highway Design award in 2002, and the American Public Works Association named the bridge the 2003 Public Works Project of the Year.

The Rattlesnake Bridge connects on a path to the Basket Bridge over Euclid Avenue south of Broadway. It is part of a pedestrian and bike path that extends to South Craycroft and East Golf Links roads.

"It represents that location where the Pantano Wash and Tanque Verde Creek merge to create the Rillito River," said Tucson artist and blacksmith David Flynn. "That's where the inspiration came from."

Brief rest

STEEL DEPICTION OF FLOWING WATER IS FOR ADMIRING, NOT SITTING

Some might take one look at the forged-steel object and judge it to be one of the most uncomfortable-looking park benches of all time.

In fact, it's public art.

The piece — titled "Reflection" — is on display along the Rillito River Park Trail just west of North Craycroft Road.

Its horizontal, ridged surface is about the height of a low park bench, but its creator said its main purpose is to be an artistic depiction of flowing water.

Installed in 2009, "It wasn't made as a bench," Tucson artist and blacksmith David Flynn said. "But I intentionally built it at that height so people could sit on it if they wanted to."

It's a fine piece of public art, perhaps best appreciated from a standing position.

It you want to see the dirty word supposedly hidden on the old Levy's building at El Con, you might want to hurry. The building was scheduled for demolition at press time for this book.

Hidden message

FORMER DEPARTMENT STORE SUPPOSEDLY HAS A SCATOLOGICAL SIDE

The vacant building on the southwest corner of El Con Mall originally housed department store Levy's when it opened in 1969.

On the upper edge of the outside wall it reads "LEVY" in a continuous cycle. Tucson folklore has it that a naughty, four-letter word can be seen by looking at the word upside down.

Turn the photo upside down and see for yourself.

The hidden message apparently was the work of a mischievous architect in the late 1960s.

"It has been a source of curiosity for many years," a chuckling mall official told the Star.

One story is that Levy's wanted a design that could be put on the exterior of the building and on shopping bags, napkins, etc., but that the first design was canned.

Then, the angered designer made the second design with the coded expletive.

The design is preserved here, as the building was scheduled for demolition when this book went to press.

Etched in stone

SANDBLASTING PRESERVED GRAFFITI TRIBUTE TO IRISH PRISONER AT UA

Who is Bobby Sands?

Inscribed on the east side of the University of Arizona's old Chemistry Building are the words "BOBBY SANDS LIVES."

The story on campus is that someone spray-painted the words on the building above the ground-floor windows in the early 1980s.

The process of removing the graffiti with a sandblaster etched it into the building and preserved it permanently.

The vandal who defaced the old Chemistry Building likely wasn't some prankster named Bobby Sands.

In May 1981, an Irish Republican Army prisoner, Bobby Sands, died on the 66th day of a hunger strike in a prison in Northern Ireland, prompting protests and demonstrations. Pro-Sands graffiti showed up across the world.

"When I first saw it, I thought it was a 'Bobby Loves Susie' type of thing," said Scott Dreisbach, laboratory manager for the Department of Chemistry and Biochemistry.

Tucson's tallest tree

EUCALYPTUS PLANTED IN 1910 ONCE SHADED MENLO PARK BUS RIDERS

Known as "Phina's Tree" — for the girl who planted it — the red gum eucalyptus hovers over the south side of West Congress Street just west of the Santa Cruz River. It is between 110 and 120 feet tall, tree experts estimate.

The eucalyptus was planted in 1910 by Delphina Valencia Lizarraga Bravo, who came to be known as "Mamaphina" after she ended up raising her nine younger siblings as a teenager.

She planted the tree to provide shade for people in the Menlo Park Neighborhood who would wait along Congress to ride the city bus.

Over the years, the tree has been maintained by the city and other groups interested in keeping its history alive. The city even altered its plans to widen Congress Street in 1970 to avoid harming Phina's Tree.

The eucalyptus was placed on the Arizona Community Tree Council's Great Trees of Arizona list in 2002 and is a regular stop on Trees for Tucson's annual Great Trees of the Old Pueblo tour.

"It's been a while since anyone's measured it, but it's definitely the biggest one in the city," said Doug Koppinger, coordinator of Trees for Tucson, part of the nonprofit agency Tucson Clean & Beautiful.